Ancient Communities: Roman Life

ANCIENT ROMAN JOBS

Nicola Barber

PowerKiDS
press.
New York

Published in 2010 by The Rosen Publishing Group Inc.
29 East 21st Street, New York, NY 10010

First Edition

Series Editor: Julia Adams
Editor: Penny Worms
Series Consultant: Sally Pointer, archaeologist
Designer: Jane Hawkins
Picture Researcher: Kathy Lockley

Library of Congress Cataloging-in-Publication Data

Barber, Nicola.
  Ancient Roman jobs / Nicola Barber.
      p. cm. -- (Ancient communities: Roman life)
  Includes index.
  ISBN 978-1-61532-307-4 (library binding)
  ISBN 978-1-61532-317-3 (paperback)
  ISBN 978-1-61532-318-0 (6-pack)
  1. Labor--Rome--Juvenile literature. 2. Working class--Rome--Juvenile literature.
  3. Occupations--Rome--Juvenile literature. I. Title.
  HD4844.B37 2010
  331.700937--dc22

                        2009023750

Photographs:
AA/The Art Archive: 27, Archaelogical Museum Istanbul/
Gianni Dagli Orti/The Art Archive: 25, Archaelogical Museum Tipasa,
Algeria/Gianni Dagli Orti/The Art Archive: 24, 28, Archaelogical Museum Venice/
Alfredo Dagli Orti/The Art Archive: 23, Jon Arnold Images/Alamy: 11Bardo Museum
Tunis/Gianni Dagli Orti/The Art Archive: 18 Mary Evans Picture Library/Alamy: 14,
Galleria Borghese, Rome/Alfredo Dagli Orti: 26 Hoberman Collection/Corbis:
COVER (inset), 10, The London Art Archive/Alamy: 7, 12, 29, Louvre, Paris,
France/Lauros/Giraudon/Bridgeman Art Library, London: 15, Marshall Ikonography/
Alamy: COVER (main), 22 Musee du Louvre, Paris/Gianni Dagli Orti/The Art Archive: 4, 17 Museo della Civilta
Romana, Rome/Gianni Dagli Orti/The Art Archive: 9 Palazzo Madama, Rome, Italy/Ancient Art & Architecture
Collection Ltd/Bridgeman Art Library, London: 8 Travelshots.com/Alamy: 6

Manufactured in China

CPSIA Compliance Information: Batch #WAW0102PK: For Further Information

contact Rosen Publishing, New York, New York at 1-800-237-9932

Contents

Words in **bold** can be found
in the glossary.

The Roman Empire

Around 2,000 years ago, the Romans controlled one of the largest and best-organized empires in history. Roman ways of life spread the length and breadth of this vast Empire.

 These are the ruins of the Forum in modern-day Rome, Italy. The Forum was the center of Rome, with shops, temples, meeting places, and law courts.

Farmers and soldiers

The Romans were originally farmers who lived in an area called Latium in the west of central Italy. The Romans extended their control across the Italian **peninsula**, and by 272 BCE, they ruled most of Italy. Roman soldiers were tough, well-trained, and disciplined, and the Romans soon began to conquer **territories** overseas. By 117 CE, the Roman Empire had reached its largest extent with territories as far north as Britain, and south to Egypt.

Republic to empire

In the early days, the Romans were ruled by a series of kings. In 509 BCE, the Romans overthrew their king. They set up a new kind of government called a **republic**, with elected leaders. The Republic came to an end in 27 BCE, when Augustus became the first Roman emperor. From this time until the fall of Rome in 476 CE, the Roman Empire was ruled by emperors.

⬆ A slave (far right) combs her mistress's hair. Many slaves worked in Roman households, cooking, cleaning, and doing other household jobs.

The Romans at work

Wherever they conquered, the Romans took their ways of life with them. Rich people were usually landowners. They kept many slaves, who were not paid for their work. Farmers were very important, because they grew the crops and raised the animals that fed the Roman people. Many other Romans had paid jobs as shopkeepers, government officials, craftworkers, doctors, lawyers, tradespeople, and entertainers.

Written at the time

In his manual on farming, *On Agriculture*, the Roman statesman, Cato the Elder, gives advice about the running of a farm and the treatment of its workers:

"Country slaves ought to receive in the winter, when they are at work, four modii [a measure of seed equal to roughly 7 quarts (8 liters)] of grain; and four modii and a half during the summer . . . slaves in chains, four pounds of bread in winter and five pounds from the time when the work of training the vines ought to begin until the figs have ripened."

Government officials

During the time of the Roman Republic, government officials called **magistrates** were elected by male **citizens** to run the government. Magistrates were not paid for their work, so only wealthy men could afford to run for election.

Magistrates

The elections for magistrates were held every year. Two magistrates were chosen to be leaders of the Republic—they were called the **consuls**. Other magistrates were put in charge of the day-to-day running of the Republic. The *praetors* looked after the law courts. The *aediles* made sure that public services, such as the water supply to Rome, were always in good condition. The *aediles* also organized public games, including chariot races and **gladiator** shows (see pages 26–27).

⬇ This painting from the 1880s imagines a scene in the Roman Senate, as the senators listen to a speaker (left).

The Senate

The Senate was another part of the Roman Republic's government system. It was made up of around 300 magistrates and ex-magistrates, called **senators**. Many senators were experienced government officials, and they advised the consuls. The Senate had a lot of power during the Republic.

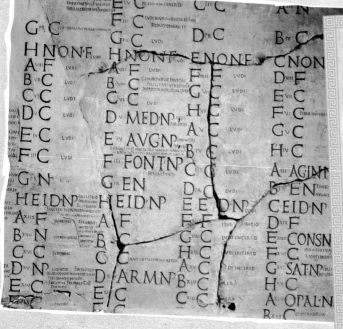

This is a Roman calendar from first century BCE.

A Roman object

The Romans used an eight-day week, and each day on this calendar is marked with a letter A to H. They later replaced the eight-day week with the seven-day week that we still use today. The Romans believed that particular days were chosen by the gods for certain activities. These days were marked on the calendar with the letters F, C, and N. F was a *dies fastus* (lawful day), when the law courts could be open. C stood for *dies comitialis*, a day when public meetings could be held. N stood for *dies nefastus* (unlawful day), when the law courts were shut and public meetings could not be held.

Tribunes

Magistrates and senators mostly came from Rome's **nobility**. These wealthy nobles were known as patricians. All other Roman citizens were known as plebeians—the common people. In the early Republic, the patricians held all the power. The plebeians elected their own representatives, called tribunes, to speak on their behalf. For many years, the plebeians and the patricians both struggled for more power. The plebeians went on strike many times, leaving the city of Rome and refusing to return until the patricians agreed to their demands.

Emperors

The emperors who ruled Rome from 27 BCE onward were very powerful. The emperor was in charge of running the Empire. He was also the commander of the Roman army.

Expanding the Empire

The Roman Empire grew with the help of many army **campaigns**. During this time, some emperors stayed in Rome and sent their trusted generals to lead the army. Others, such as Emperor Trajan, spent long periods of their reign away from Rome leading their armies themselves. Trajan was so successful as a general that by the time of his death in 117 CE, the Roman Empire was at its largest.

Augustus the wise

Emperor Augustus ruled from 31 BCE to 14 CE. He introduced many changes to the Roman Empire. Once he had seized power, he started to reorganize the rebuilding of large parts of Rome. He also introduced a fire department and a police force in the city. Augustus brought about a time of peace that was known as the *Pax Romana*. He became very popular with the Roman people, and after his death, he was declared a god.

⬆ This gold coin shows Emperor Augustus. Augustus's family name was Caesar, from Julius Caesar.

This is a scene from Trajan's Column in Rome. The column was built to celebrate the victories of Emperor Trajan.

Chief priest

Augustus, and the emperors that followed him, also acted as *Pontifex Maximus* (high priest). Before the time of Augustus, the high priest was elected. Augustus took the title *Pontifex Maximus* in 13 BCE after the death of the last elected high priest. The *Pontifex Maximus* was in charge of important matters, such as the Roman calendar (see page 9), and overseeing religious law. The title gave the emperor great religious power.

Claudius
10 BCE–54 CE

Claudius became emperor in 41 CE when his uncle, Emperor Caligula, was murdered. He did not have a lot of military experience, so people thought he was not the right person to be an emperor. He decided that a military victory would make him more popular with the people of Rome. That is why he ordered an invasion of Britain. He himself traveled to Britain when it became clear that the Roman campaign had been a success.

Roman soldiers

The Romans created one of the most successful armies in history. Roman soldiers were well-trained and highly disciplined. They were fearsome opponents in battle.

The legionary

The basic unit of the Roman army was the legion, a group of roughly 6,000 soldiers called legionaries. The legionaries were all Roman citizens. They were mostly foot soldiers, although wealthy men who could afford the equipment could join as **cavalrymen** on horseback. Early in Roman history, the legionaries were called up for service when they were needed. At the end of each campaign, they returned home to their normal lives. As Roman power grew, there was a need for a permanent army. By the late Republic, being a legionary was a full-time, paid job.

 These soldiers are members of the Praetorian Guard. Their job was to guard the emperor.

Written at the time

This account of the Roman army was written by the Jewish historian, Josephus, in around 75 CE. It describes the equipment carried by a legionary on the march:

"... the foot soldiers [legionaries] have a spear and a long buckler [shield], besides a saw and a basket, a pickax, and an ax, a thong of leather and a hook, with provisions for three days ..."

The auxiliary

As the Romans expanded their territories overseas, the army began to recruit noncitizen soldiers to fight alongside the legionaries. These noncitizen soldiers were called auxiliaries. The auxiliary soldiers often had special skills. Some were good horsemen who fought on horseback, and others used slings or bows and arrows as their weapons. However, auxiliaries were paid much less than the legionaries.

Hadrian's Wall, in the north of England, was built by Roman legionaries to prevent attacks from the tribes to the north. You can see the remains of one of the forts along the wall, where the legionaries lived.

A varied life

As well as being skilled fighters, Roman legionaries and auxiliaries were also trained to perform many other important jobs. They built their own camps and forts. They also built roads and bridges. By the first century CE, the Romans had conquered much of their Empire, so the soldiers' main task was to defend it. Roman soldiers lived in all parts of the Empire, patrolling its borders, and putting down **uprisings**.

Priests and priestesses

People across the Roman Empire believed in many different gods. Priests, and some priestesses, led the worship of these gods.

Priests

Most priests were important men in public life who held the office of priesthood as one of their many public duties. They pulled their togas over their heads in order to show that they were acting as priests. Priests led the worship of the gods and goddesses. There were also priests called *augurs*. They tried to understand the will of the gods by looking at signs in the natural world, such as the flight of birds.

 These Roman augurs are watching the behavior of some hens to try understand the will of the gods.

Worship

The Romans built temples to be the homes of particular gods and goddesses. It was the priest's job to look after the temple. People gathered outside a temple to pray and to make **offerings** to the god or goddess. There were often animal **sacrifices**. Once the animal was dead, the priest burned some of its organs as an offering to the gods. The rest of the meat was often cooked and eaten by the priest and worshipers.

⬆ These animals are about to be sacrificed to Mars, the Roman god of war.

A Roman object

This sculpture was carved onto a monument built by a consul called Domitius Ahenobarbus in around 100 BCE. It shows a sacrifice to Mars, the god of war. One of the priests has pulled his toga over his head. Others are wearing crowns of laurel leaves. They are leading a bull, a ram, and a pig to an altar where the animals will be sacrificed.

Vestal Virgins

Most priests were men, but the Vestal Virgins were priestesses who looked after the temple of Vesta in Rome. Vesta was the goddess who watched over the hearth. A fire burned continuously inside her temple in Rome, tended by the six Vestal Virgins. These women were chosen by the high priest when they were girls, and it was considered a great honor. They served as priestesses for 30 years, during which time they were not allowed to marry.

Women's work

Roman women did not have an official role in public life, although some had a great deal of power and influence. Women were mostly expected to run their households and bring up their children.

Roman marriage

In Roman times, girls were often married very young. By law, girls were allowed to marry when they were 12 years old, and it was common for fathers to choose husbands for their daughters. The main purpose of marriage was to produce children, particularly boys, to continue the **family line**. In rich families, marriages were often arranged for **political** or **financial** reasons.

This is an illustration of a scene inside a house in Pompeii, Italy. It shows Roman women writing and caring for their children.

Running the household

Married women looked after the running of the household and controlled the finances. The households of wealthy Romans were busy places, with many slaves living and working there. Some women helped to run large estates. It was a woman's job to make clothes for her family. This involved spinning wool or linen to make yarn, and weaving the cloth. Women also brought up their children, and taught their daughters the skills they would need to run their own households.

Outside the home

Some women worked outside the home. There were female **midwives** and nurses, and others took on jobs such as sewing or washing clothes. Some women ran shops or bars, and there were also a few female doctors. There were many women slaves, with jobs such as farm work or hairdressing.

Livia Drusilla
58 BCE–29 CE

Livia Drusilla was the wife of Emperor Augustus (see page 10). She was a very powerful woman, even though she could not take an official part in public life. She was devoted to her husband, but she had two sons by an earlier marriage, and she was ruthless in her ambitions for them. Some Roman historians think she was responsible for the deaths of many of her sons' rivals. When Augustus died in 14 CE, Livia's eldest son, Tiberius, became emperor.

As the wife of Emperor Augustus, Livia Drusilla was a powerful and ambitious woman.

Tradesmen

Trade flourished during the Roman Empire, as huge amounts of goods were transported by sea and over land. Across the Empire, most people used Roman coins to buy and sell goods.

Supplying Rome

The city of Rome had a huge population—it is possible that more than one million people lived in the city when it was most powerful. All these people needed food and goods, and trade with Rome was important for **merchants** from all over the Empire. During the summer months, when it was safe for ships to sail the seas, cargoes of wheat, wine, olive oil, and a type of fish sauce called *garum* arrived at the mouth of the River Tiber. Slaves unloaded the ships, and the goods were taken to huge warehouses in Rome.

 These slaves are unloading a cargo of iron ore off a ship and weighing it.

Exotic trade

The Romans built roads across the Empire so that their soldiers could march quickly from one place to another. The roads also allowed traders and merchants to travel. Chinese silk was very popular with rich Romans, and it was imported from China along a route called the Silk Road. Merchants and traders also brought precious gems and spices, such as pepper, cloves, and cinnamon, from India. These goods were transported by ship across the Indian Ocean and through the Red Sea.

Markets and shops

Merchants sold their goods in shops and markets. General goods, such as clothes, were available at the Forum Cuppedinis. Rome's cattle market was the Forum Boarium, and vegetables were sold at the Forum Holitorium. There was also a wine market, a pork market, and a fish market.

A Roman object

Amphorae were used by the Romans to transport all kinds of goods including wine, olive oil, garum, olives, fish, and grain. They were made all over the Roman Empire. Many amphorae had pointed ends so that they could be packed tightly together in the hold of a ship. Ropes were threaded through the handles to stop the amphorae moving around during a rough crossing.

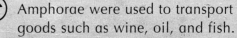
Amphorae were used to transport goods such as wine, oil, and fish.

Craftworkers

We know from the beautiful objects that have survived from Roman times that there were many highly skilled craftworkers in the Roman Empire. They included metalworkers, jewelry makers, glassmakers, and potters.

Metalwork

Most Roman towns and cities had small workshops for metalworking. The Romans used iron and bronze (a mixture of copper and tin).The metalworker heated the metal and then hammered it into shapes to make items such as armor and knives. Some metalworkers made highly decorated objects and jewelry out of silver or gold for wealthy clients.

These gold earrings were made by an Roman metalworker. The beads are made from glass.

Glassmakers

Glassmaking was an important craft in Roman times. Glassmakers knew how to make a wide variety of objects including bottles and jars, beads, **mosaics,** and windows. The art of blowing **molten** glass into bubbles to create hollow shapes was discovered some time in the first century BCE. This technique was used by craftworkers in the Roman Empire to make bottles and flasks of all kinds.

This glass beaker comes from Pompeii in Italy.

A Roman object

Glass beakers were made by blowing hot glass into a mold, which was usually made of clay. The mold of this beaker had the decoration on the inside, and the hot glass flowed in to take on the shape and pattern of the mold. When the glass had cooled down and hardened, the glassmaker removed the mold, to be used again. Mold-blowing was a very common way of producing decorated glass objects in Roman times.

Pottery

Potters used clay to make everyday items, such as bowls and cups, jugs and oil lamps. A type of pottery with a shiny, red finish became very popular. This pottery was made in large factories in Arezzo, Italy, and near Lyon in France. Pottery was used by people all over the Roman Empire for eating and drinking.

Farmers

Most people in the Roman world lived and worked in the countryside. Farming provided the food that was needed by the huge population of the Roman Empire.

Landowners and slaves

Farms ranged in size from large estates to smallholdings. The estates, called *latifundia*, were owned by rich Roman nobles, and were passed down from one **generation** to the next. Most landowners spent much of their time in the towns. They visited their estates only to go hunting, and during the summer months, to escape the heat of the towns. The actual farm work was done by teams of slaves. It was backbreaking work for these men, women, and children.

 This Roman floor mosaic shows one slave driving an oxcart while another pulls the oxen forward.

Animals and crops

Some farms specialized in raising animals or growing particular crops. There were large cattle ranches and sheep farms. Some farmers grew vegetables or olives, and others grew cereal crops, such as wheat. Nearly all of the work was done by hand. Since the Romans had so many slaves, they did not bother to develop many **labor-saving devices**.

Vineyards

Some farms grew vines for wine-making. Wine was a very important drink in the Roman Empire, because the Romans did not have tea or coffee. Looking after vines was hard work. The vines had to be tied up to supports, pruned, and the grapes picked, all at the right times.

Written at the time

This extract from *De Agricultura* (On Agriculture; c.160 BCE) by Marcus Cato describes the ideal site for a farm:

"It should have a good climate, not subject to storms; the soil should be good, and naturally strong. If possible, it should lie at the foot of a mountain and face south; the situation should be healthful, there should be a good supply of laborers, it should be well watered, and near it there should be a flourishing town, or the sea, or a navigable stream, or a good and much-traveled road."

 These two men are stamping on a container of grapes to release their juice to make wine. The man on the far left is about to add another basket of grapes.

23

Slaves

Slaves were usually prisoners of war. They were brought to Italy to be sold at the slave markets. The Romans relied on the work of slaves in their homes, on their farms, and in their towns and cities.

Prisoners of war such as these were often taken back to Rome as slaves.

Life as a slave

Many slaves worked in their owners' houses, cooking, cleaning, washing, and attending to all their owners' needs. Some of these slaves had relatively comfortable lives, and some were even thought of as members of the family. Most slaves could not read or write, but some slaves, particularly those who came from Greece, were well educated. These slaves often worked as secretaries, teachers, or **scribes**.

Farm slaves

The many thousands of slaves who worked on large farming estates, or in the mines, were not as fortunate as house servants. Farm slaves were often treated badly and not given enough food. Many slaves died as a result. Some slaves were forced to wear iron collars with the details of their owners carved onto the metal, in case they tried to escape.

⬆ These slaves have been linked together with collars to prevent them from escaping.

Freedom

Slaves could become freedmen or freedwomen. Sometimes owners paid slaves for their work, so they could save up enough money to buy their freedom. Some owners gave slaves their freedom as a thank you for their work. Most freed slaves became Roman citizens. They often continued to work for their old masters.

Spartacus
109 BCE–71 BCE

Spartacus was from Greece. He was caught and sold as a slave. In 73 BCE, he escaped with about 80 other slaves and set up camp on Mount Vesuvius. Other runaways joined the slaves, until Spartacus led an army of about 70,000 **rebels**. The rebels defeated the Roman army and took control of much of southern Italy. The rebellion lasted until 71 BCE, when Spartacus was killed in battle and the Roman army defeated the rebels.

Fighters and charioteers

Some slaves were chosen to train to become fighters, called gladiators. Like chariot racing, gladiator fights were very popular.

Life as a gladiator

As well as slaves, convicted criminals and prisoners of war were sent to gladiator schools to be trained. Life at gladiator school was very tough, but the food was good because the gladiators needed to be fit and healthy to fight well. Some gladiators became celebrities. If a gladiator had a successful career, he could be rewarded for his skill and bravery with a wooden sword. This showed that he no longer had to fight.

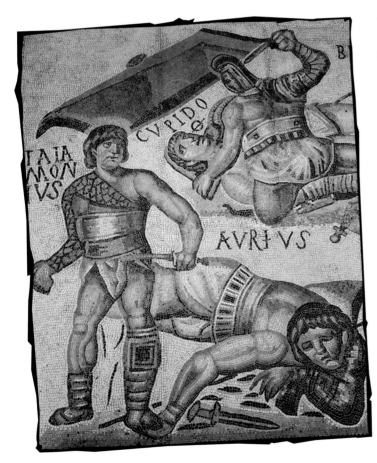

Kinds of gladiator

There were many different kinds of gladiator, who used different armor and weapons. The *hoplomachus* wore heavy protective armor and used a short, stabbing sword to attack his opponent. The *murmillo* often fought the *hoplomachus*. The *retarius* was armed with a net and a trident (a three-pronged spear). He often fought against a *secutor*, who wore a smooth, egg-shaped helmet and carried a small sword.

 These gladiators are fighting at a game. Gladiators used many kinds of weapon and armor.

Written at the time

Scorpus was a famous charioteer who won over 2,000 victories during his short life. He was killed, probably in a crash at a race, at a young age. In his "Epigrams" books, the Roman poet, Martial, wrote this about Scorpus:

"I am Scorpus, the idol of the noisy Circus,
The much-applauded but short-lived darling of Rome,
Envious Fate, counting my victories instead of my years,
and so believing me old, carried me off in my
twenty-sixth year."

Chariot racing

People in the Roman world went to their local **amphitheater** to watch gladiator fights. They visited the nearest circus (racetrack) to watch chariot racing. Both were very popular. Like gladiators, successful charioteers were treated like stars. Most charioteers were slaves, or ex-slaves, but some became rich and famous from the gifts they received from wealthy admirers.

This mosaic shows a charioteer driving a four-horse chariot during a race.

Timeline

Glossary

amphitheater an oval-shaped, open-air building with an arena in the center surrounded by seats

campaign a series of battles that form part of a plan to achieve a specific goal

cavalrymen soldiers trained to fight on horseback

citizens in Roman times, a citizen was originally a resident of Rome itself, but later people all over the Roman Empire became Roman citizens

consuls a consul was one of two heads of state during the Roman Republic

family line the ancestors of a family

financial to do with money

generation a group of people who are all about the same age

labor-saving devices machines or other objects that help to reduce the amount of effort put in by people

magistrates government officials of the Roman Empire

merchants people who trade goods

midwives a woman who attended the birth of a baby

molten red-hot and liquidlike

mosaics designs or pictures that are made with small pieces of colored glass or stone

nobility a class of wealthy and high-born people

noncitizen a person in the territories conquered by the Romans

offerings gifts offered to a god or goddess as part of a religious ceremony

political connected to the ruling of a country

rebels people who rebel against the government

republic a kind of government in which the citizens elect officials to represent them

sacrifices animals that were killed as an offering to the gods during religious ceremonies

scribes people whose job is to write things down

senators members of the Senate, the group of men who advised the consuls, and later the emperor

territories areas under the control of a foreign power

uprisings revolts or rebellions

Index

Resources and Web Sites

People of the Ancient World: The Ancient Romans by Allison Lassieur (Children's Press, 2005)

Rich and Poor in Ancient Rome by Richard Dargie (Smart Apple Media, 2005)

You Wouldn't Want to be a Roman Gladiator! by John Malam (Scholastic Library, 2001)

Web Sites

Due to the changing nature of Internet links, PowerKids Press has developed an online list of Web sites related to the subject of this book. This site is updated regularly. Please use this link to access this list:
http://www.powerkidslinks.com/acrl/jobs/